SPORTS ZONE

# FOOTBALL

## A Guide for Players and Fans

BY MATT CHANDLER

CAPSTONE PRESS
a capstone imprint

Fact Finders Books are published by Capstone
1710 Roe Crest Drive, North Mankato, Minnesota 56003
www.capstonepub.com

**Editorial Credits**

Lauren Dupuis-Perez, editor; Sara Radka, designer;
Eric Gohl, media researcher; Laura Manthe, production specialist

**Photo Credits**

Getty Images: Allsport/Stephen Dunn, 12, Corey Jenkins, 10-11, Erik
Isakson, 20, GeorgePeters, 11 (foreground), 23, Harry How, cover
(front), 24, Hero Images, cover (background), Jose Luis Palaez Inc, 28,
Meg Oliphant, 29 (top), Norm Hall, 17, 19, OSTILL, 22, Otto Greule
Jr, 29 (bottom), Patrick Smith, 27, Pete Starman, 8-9, Ronald Martinez,
4, Steven Ryan, 25; Newscom: Cal Sport Media/Chris Szagola, 14,
Icon Sportswire CGV/Rich Graessle, 13, Southcreek Global/Philippe
Champoux, 18; Pixabay: intographics, background; Wikimedia:
Courtesy of the Gerald R. Ford Presidential Museum, 9 (bottom), The
University of the South (Sewanee), 7 (top), Unknown, 6, 7 (bottom),
9 (top)

**Library of Congress Cataloging-in-Publication Data**

Names: Chandler, Matt author.
Title: Football : a guide for players and fans / by Matt Chandler.
Description: North Mankato, Minnesota : Capstone Press, [2019] |
Series: Fact Finders. Sports Zone | Audience: Age 8-9. | Audience: K
to grade 3.
Identifiers: LCCN 2019005979 | ISBN 9781543573572 (Hardcover) |
ISBN 9781543574562 (Paperback) | ISBN 9781543573695 (eBook PDF)
Subjects: LCSH: Football—United States—Juvenile literature. |
Football for children—United States—Juvenile literature.
Classification: LCC GV950.7 .C53 2019 | DDC 796.332—dc23
LC record available at https://lccn.loc.gov/2019005979

# TABLE OF CONTENTS

# INTRODUCTION

Quarterback Tom Brady has played for the New England Patriots since joining the NFL in 2000.

Tom Brady had already won four Super Bowl rings and was considered one of the greatest quarterbacks of all time. But on February 5, 2017, none of that seemed to matter. The Atlanta Falcons defense was pressuring the New England Patriots quarterback on every play. The Falcons held a 28–3 lead halfway through the third quarter of Super Bowl LI.

With more than 111 million people watching, Brady staged the greatest comeback in Super Bowl history. Brady forced overtime by leading his team to 25 points in the second half. He also set a Super Bowl record with 466 yards passing. The future Pro Football Hall of Famer completed five straight passes on an overtime drive. Brady had his team two yards away from earning his fifth Super Bowl ring. Time was running short. Brady pitched the ball to running back James White. He dove for the end zone, and the Patriots were world champions!

Jim Thorpe was one of football's most famous players in the early 20th century. He became the first president of the NFL.

More than 103,000 fans packed the Rose Bowl on January 20, 1980, to watch Super Bowl XIV. It set the record for the largest crowd in the history of professional football. But it wasn't always that way. Only about 100 fans watched Rutgers and Princeton play the first college football game in 1869.

Football originally gained popularity on college campuses around the country. The sport was changed forever with the formation of the National Football League (NFL) in 1920.

In the beginning pro football players were paid as little as $100 per game. Halfback Red Grange of the Chicago Bears signed the first large contract in 1925. It was worth $100,000. That would be equal to more than $1.4 million today! Currently there are 32 NFL teams that play a 16-game regular season schedule. The average NFL player earned more than $2 million in 2018!

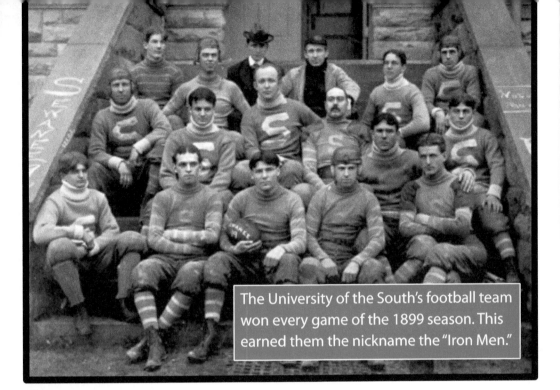

The University of the South's football team won every game of the 1899 season. This earned them the nickname the "Iron Men."

## "Pudge" Gets Paid

Football began as an amateur game with young athletes playing for the love of competition. That all changed on November 12, 1892. The Allegheny Athletic Association added a few new players to its team. William "Pudge" Heffelfinger was one of the players. He was paid $500 to play in the game, making him the first professional football player. Pudge earned his money. His fumble return for a touchdown was the only score in the game.

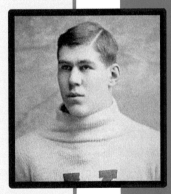

amateur — describes a sports league that athletes take part in for pleasure rather than for money
fumble — when a player drops the ball or it is knocked out of his or her hands by another player

The Pro Football Hall of Fame in Canton, Ohio, honors football's best players.

Only 318 players have earned the Gold Jacket and a spot in the Hall of Fame. The Hall of Fame is also a museum documenting the history of the game. Fans can see items from players who may never make the Hall of Fame. David Tyree is an example of such a player. Tyree caught only 54 passes in his career. But one of these catches took place in Super Bowl XLII against the New England Patriots and earned his helmet a spot in the Hall of Fame. With the game on the line, Tyree made an amazing one-handed catch, pulling the ball in and holding it against his helmet as he crashed to the ground. The "Helmet Catch" led the New York Giants to a game-winning touchdown and an NFL championship.

Gold Jacket — a special gold-colored coat given to players inducted into the Pro Football Hall of Fame

1869

1920

1936

1958

1967

The first college football game is played. Rutgers defeats Princeton 6–4.

The National Football League is formed in Canton, Ohio. The league has 14 teams in its first season of play.

The first NFL draft of college players is held on February 8, 1936. Chicago halfback Jay Berwanger is the first player ever drafted.

The Canadian Football League (CFL) plays its first season. The Winnipeg Blue Bombers defeat the Hamilton Tiger-Cats 35–28 to win the championship.

## BACON BALLS

Footballs are referred to as "pigskins" even though most are made of cowhide. In the early days of the game, many footballs were made from pig bladders. Yuck!

Super Bowl I is played on January 15, 1967. It is known as the AFL-NFL World Championship. The Green Bay Packers defeat the Kansas City Chiefs 35–10.

# FOOTBALL GEAR

Modern football players take the field with their bodies protected by the best equipment available. Equipment has come a long way from the first college football game in 1869. Safety was the last thing on anyone's mind when Rutgers and Princeton took the field. Players wore regular clothes. The helmet hadn't been invented. Rutgers players wrapped colorful scarfs around their heads so they could easily spot fellow teammates. Pants were held up by suspenders, and players didn't wear shoulder pads. Protecting players became more important as the game became more popular.

### 1. Helmets
The first leather helmets were used in the early 1890s. Helmets were optional until 1943.

### 2. Cleats
Cleats began as a way to help players run faster. They help players grip the grass or turf.

### 3. Shoulder Pads
Quarterbacks and kickers wear small shoulder pads. Today players strive to wear the lightest shoulder pads possible.

### 4. Mouthgaurds
A 200-pound (90-kilogram) cornerback hitting a wide receiver can deliver more than 1,600 pounds (725 kg) of tackling force. Mouthguards help protect players' teeth.

### 5. Padded Pants
Protective pads were sewn into football pants as early as the late 1880s. Padding helps protect players from violent hits.

## Safety vs. Speed

In the 1980s, running back Herschel Walker ran through the middle of the defense and hit defensive players before they hit him. It helped that running backs such as Walker wore extra-large shoulder pads. The pads protected players against punishing hits. Many players felt like bulky equipment slowed them down.

Walker rushed for more than 8,000 yards as a pro. In the years since then, equipment companies have found a balance between safety and comfort. Today, New York Giants running back Saquon Barkley wears pads much smaller than what Walker wore. Now players are lighter and still protected against many injuries.

Herschel Walker played for the Philadelphia Eagles and three other teams during his NFL career, which spanned 12 seasons.

There is plenty of optional safety equipment as well. Hall of Fame QB "Broadway Joe" Namath had a history of knee injuries while in college. After being drafted by the New York Jets, Namath wore a bulky knee brace for a full season. The brace helped protect Namath from defenders diving at his legs. Namath stayed healthy and led his Jets to victory in Super Bowl III. It was such an important piece of equipment that Namath's knee brace joined the QB in the Hall of Fame!

## Head Health

On January 23, 1994, Dallas Cowboys quarterback Troy Aikman dropped back to pass. As San Francisco 49ers defender Dennis Brown sacked Aikman, he drove his knee against Aikman's helmet. The star QB suffered a concussion. Aikman has no memory of ever playing the game.

Today technology has improved helmets. The rules have also changed. Defenders can't lead with their heads when tackling. Hits to the head are also against the rules.

concussion — an injury to the brain caused by a hard blow to the head

# RULES OF THE GAME

In the 2018 season, most penalties were called for offensive holding and false starts.

The New England Patriots played the Oakland Raiders in the divisional round of the 2001 NFL playoffs. Raiders cornerback Charles Woodson sacked Patriots QB Tom Brady in the fourth quarter. The ball came loose. The Raiders recovered and appeared ready to win the game. The officials talked it over. An obscure rule known as the "Tuck Rule" turned the fumble into an incompletion. The Patriots went on to win the game and won the first of five Super Bowl titles under head coach Bill Belichick.

Football has a lot of rules. Understanding the basic rules is critical to following the game. Each team is allowed 11 players on the field. One important rule involves understanding offsides. Players can't cross the line of scrimmage before the ball is snapped. Another rule protects players trying to catch the ball. Defenders who hit the receiver before the football arrives can be penalized for pass interference.

incompletion — in football, a pass that is not caught by a player
scrimmage — the imaginary line where a play begins

## Rules for Defense

The rules of the game have made football hard on defensive players. With a rise in concussions, the rules have changed to protect players. Defenders trying to sack the quarterback are now penalized for hits to the head or the knees. Receivers are also protected. Rules don't allow a defender to hit a receiver who is "defenseless." The NFL added and revised these and other rules to protect players before the 2018 season. That led to a record number of touchdowns being scored. Offensive players appreciate the new rules. Defenders like 49ers cornerback Richard Sherman aren't fans. Asked in an interview about the change in rules, the All-Pro said, "They're just trying to make it impossible for guys to play defense." The league continues to adjust the game to prevent harming players.

All-Pro — an honor given to players voted the league's best player at their position

Richard Sherman (center) made 30 solo tackles for the San Francisco 49ers during the 2018 season.

Damon Duval was named a Canadian Football League All-Star in 2011.

## Special Teams, Special Rules

The Saskatchewan Roughriders led the Montreal Alouettes 27–25 with no time on the clock in the 2009 CFL championship. Montreal had one chance at a game-winning field goal, but Damon Duval's kick sailed wide to the right. The game was over . . . or was it? The Roughriders were penalized for having too many men on the field. Duval was given another chance. His second kick was perfect. One rule violation cost a team the championship!

Many rules on NFL special teams are designed to keep players safe. When returning a kick or a punt, a player can signal for a fair catch by waving his hand over his head. The defenders can't tackle the player, and he can't advance the ball.

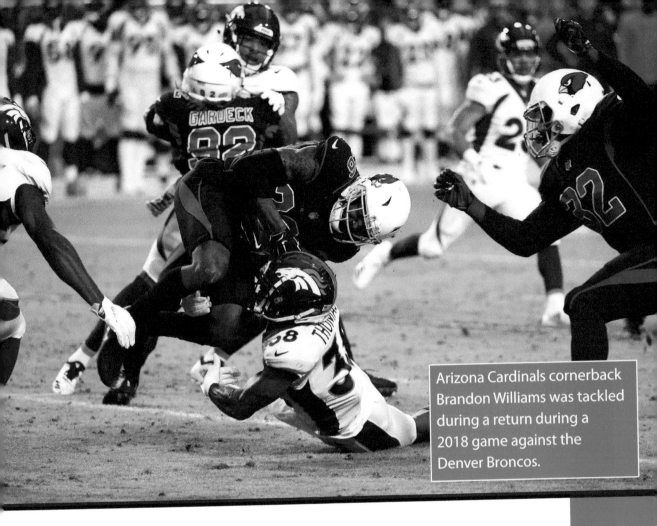

Arizona Cardinals cornerback Brandon Williams was tackled during a return during a 2018 game against the Denver Broncos.

The NFL added a new rule in 2018 for kickoffs. The kicking team used to get a running start. Now, they must stand still until the ball is kicked. This reduces the speed they are traveling when they tackle the ball carrier.

## SPIKE IT!

Professional football players celebrate touchdowns by spiking the ball in the end zone. College players aren't allowed to celebrate with a spike. Such celebrations are considered poor sportsmanship and result in a penalty.

# STRATEGIES TO SUCCEED

An estimated 3 million children ages 6 to 18 play football in the United States.

As a young player just starting out, how do you decide what position to play? Usually it comes down to trying out different roles on a team to see what you like. There are some guidelines. Running backs are usually fast and can take getting hit a lot. Wide receivers have great hands and can make tough catches. Quarterbacks are usually tall. That helps them see over the defenders rushing toward them. They also need a strong arm to make deep throws down the field. Because they run the offense, the quarterback is often one of the smartest players on the field.

Where you play on the football field can also come down to your coach knowing what you do best. Football is a sport where every player has a chance to make an impact.

## Winning off the Field

Football players practice for hours to perfect their skills. Field goal kickers drill hundreds of balls through the uprights in practice. Running backs run through a tunnel of teammates who pound at them to try and knock the ball loose. Quarterbacks practice thousands of passes during a season to get the timing perfect with their receivers.

Players at every level of football must be in excellent physical condition. Teams run wind sprints and aerobic exercises. Kickers work to stretch their legs. Wide receivers run sprints in preparation for running as many as 30 to 40 pass patterns in a game.

Running backs must have powerful legs that give them a burst of speed off the line of scrimmage. They also must be quick on their feet and able to avoid tackles.

Sam Adams (95) played in the NFL's all-star game, the Pro Bowl, three times during his career, in 2000, 2001, and 2004.

Buffalo Bills defensive end Sam Adams didn't look like a traditional athlete. Adams weighed 350 pounds (159 kg) and wasn't known for his speed. But in 2003, Adams intercepted a pass in his team's home opener and rumbled 40 yards into the end zone. Adams worked hard on his conditioning to be ready for that type of situation.

aerobic exercise — racing long distances at medium speed
conditioning — training your body to be better able to handle the demands of fitness and sports

The Philadelphia Eagles' Nick Foles was named MVP of Super Bowl LII for his performance as quarterback.

## Field Strategy

Fans sometimes see football players as tackling machines. But a lot goes into making a tackle. The hard work begins long before a player touches an opponent. On-field strategies help put players in the right positions to make plays.

Quarterbacks must look over the defense before they hike the ball. If they see a slow linebacker covering a wide receiver, they change the play to take advantage of the uneven matchup.

Linebackers try to read the quarterback's eyes to see where he is looking to throw the ball. Then they can "jump the route" and get in front of the receiver for an interception.

Players on special teams use strategies to decide what route to take on a punt return or whether or not to return a kickoff out of the end zone. A football player uses his brain as much as his body on every play.

A wide receiver for the Houston Texans, DeAndre Carter returned 26 punts for a total 249 yards in 2018.

# READY TO PLAY?

Some of today's best players began on the playground with a pickup game of two-hand touch. Playground ball is a great way to learn the game. What's it like to be a quarterback? How hard is it to catch a deep ball over your shoulder? Is it scary to return a punt with an entire team chasing you? The unique rules of playground ball don't always match up with organized football rules. Touch football is different from tackling a player. Sandlot football is still an awesome way to develop a love for the game and prepare a young player to join a team.

When you are ready to take the next step, there is flag football. The NFL runs a program with more than 1,000 flag football leagues across the United States. These leagues offer more structure and coaching, but without the tackling.

In flag football, players try to pull the flag from their opponents' belts instead of tackling.

## From Pop Warner to the Pros

When you are confident you like the sport, Pop Warner Little Scholars is the ultimate youth tackle football league. The youth football league was named for a famous coach and dates back to 1929. Since then, Pop Warner football has been a training ground for thousands of football players. More than 325,000 youth play Pop Warner football, cheer, and dance in the United States. There are 5,000 teams across the country. For some children, it is the perfect level of football to enjoy. For others, it is a starting point on the road to a career as a football player. The path you choose is up to you. No matter what level you play at, the game of football is fast, fun, and challenging. Someone picking up this book may go on to play in high school, college, or even the NFL!

More than 60 percent of NFL players got their start playing Pop Warner football.

### KICK-START YOUR CAREER

There is one unique way to get started as a football player—start with soccer. Most field goal kickers kick with the side of their foot, "soccer style."

Some football camps focus on a particular position, such as the Steve Clarkson Quarterback Camps in California.

## Summer Camp

Summer football camps are a great place to improve your skills. Hall of Fame quarterback Peyton Manning's academy has trained thousands of young players. Summer programs stress the **fundamentals** of the game. Good sportsmanship is also part of many camps. Do football camps help? Ask Russell Wilson. The Seattle Seahawks quarterback attended the Manning Passing Academy as a teen. Wilson is a five-time Pro Bowl player who led the NFL in passing touchdowns in 2017!

fundamental—a basic idea or necessary part

# Glossary

**aerobic exercise** *(ayr-OH-bik EK-suhr-syz)*—racing long distances at medium speed

**All-Pro** *(AWL-PRO)*—an honor given to players voted the league's best player at their position

**amateur** *(AM-uh-chur)*—describes a sports league that athletes take part in for pleasure rather than for money

**concussion** *(kuhn-KUH-shuhn)*—an injury to the brain caused by a hard blow to the head

**conditioning** *(kuhn-DI-shuhn-ing)*—training your body to be better able to handle the demands of fitness and sports

**fumble** *(FUHM-buhl)*—when a player drops the ball or it is knocked out of his or her hands by another player

**fundamental** *(fuhn-duh-MEN-tuhl)*—a basic idea or necessary part

**Gold Jacket** *(GOLD JAK-et)*—a special gold-colored coat given to players inducted into the Pro Football Hall of Fame

**incompletion** *(in-kuhm-PLEE-shun)*—in football, a pass that is not caught by a player

**scrimmage** *(SKRIM-ij)*—the imaginary line where a play begins

# Read More

**Frederick, Shane.** *Stars of the Super Bowl.* Everything Super Bowl. North Mankato, MN: Capstone Press, 2017.

**Gramling, Gary.** *The Football Fanbook.* New York: Liberty Street, 2017.

**Jacobs, Greg.** *The Everything Kids' Football Book.* Avon, MA: Adams Media, 2018.

# Internet Sites

*National Football League*
www.nfl.com

*Pro Football Hall of Fame*
www.profootballhof.com

*NFL Play 60 Movement*
www.nfl.com/play60

# Index